T0147394

Finally At Ease With Myself

William J. Houston

iUniverse, Inc.
New York   Bloomington

Finally At Ease With Myself

This is a work of fiction. All of the characters, names, incidents, organizations, and dialogue in this novel are either the products of the author's imagination or are used fictitiously.

iUniverse books may be ordered through booksellers or by contacting:

iUniverse
1663 Liberty Drive
Bloomington, IN 47403
www.iuniverse.com
1-800-Authors (1-800-288-4677)

ISBN: 978-1-4401-1170-9 (sc)
ISBN: 978-1-4401-1171-6 (ebook)

Printed in the United States of America

iUniverse rev. date: 2/5/2009

Cover Design by Ty Houston

Dedication

To my mother who gave me life,

*To my father "Ducky" who
taught me about life,*

To my son who is my life.

Foreword

It seems that my life has crested now and what has flowed past has been some what turmoil. The early stages of my life were filled with confusion. It seemed like everything around me was functioning normal except for my life. This caused some great concern on my behalf leaving me wondering was there actually peace in this world.

The years of adolescent innocence were just that -- innocent and naive. I really felt a need to belong but to what. I didn't think it was family. These feelings were greatly influenced and supported by the mere fact that I never really felt like I belonged to a family when I was growing up. It 's more like I was on loan to this relative or that one or until the time was suitable for me to be passed again. In desperation, I reached out to anything that offered me the feeling of belonging. The military was perfect for me. I belonged to something that was willing to accept me for who I was. For the most part, it was an excellent thing, and I was disciplined and trained. Later on in life, I realized that my turmoil of emotions was just what they were looking for and they capitalized on it for all it was worth. The years following the military were an even greater mass of confusion in my mind. This alone caused the destruction of my marriage and me, even more withdrawal from the norms. I just kept going forward and tried to focus on the future and my son. Along the way, I found contempt for things and because of this, I started to write. So here I am now feeling pretty good about myself and letting the world know how I feel. I don't know if it was this easy all along, but I do know that I am At Ease with my life now.

Table of Contents

WAR

It came from the darkness of the mind,
thoughts placed there are so sublime.
Like a mill worm, it gnawed a tiny hole,
and poured out, ever so slow.

It seeped into the reality of life,
causing havoc and strife.
It was a disease without a cure,
touching the whole world leaving nothing pure.

All succumbed to its ravenous needs,
as it spreads like wildflower from seeds.
Its face was the same as before,
and is easily identified as war

Words of a Letter

I wrote the letter again today,
and again I threw it away,
Will I ever find the right words, I wonder,
ones written perfect without a blunder.

They have to be right, deeply expressed,
for the subject matter of death is addressed.
A standard letter is supplied for the ones,
who don't have the heart to describe loss sons.

I cannot disrespect them like that,
or the ones waiting for bodies sent back.
I have to tell them that they weren't alone,
when the moment came so far from home.

They need to be told, the goodness of a son,
and how I wish I could of been the one,
for it was I who gave orders for harm's way,
and that I must live with every day.

It cannot be just a form or repeated sentiment,
but words that come from the heart and are intimate.
I must express my love for him, for he was my child,
for whom I was entrusted, to protect with unrelenting guild.

They must feel from these words, my failure to do so,
not just by me saying, but by the written emotional flow,
which describes my sadness and my plea for forgiveness,
for I know I have violated all hope of trustfulness.

My words must put them at ease,
and soothe the souls that need pleased.
In those words I must find tranquility,
and describe it to the best of my ability.

So I write the letter again,
and with each stroke of the pen,
I strive for the right words to make amends,
impossible, when describing when a son's life ends.

The Red Ribbon

The voice of the mail orderly was weak,
as he hollered the names last week.
I strained my ears to hear my name,
hoping that the results wouldn't be the same.

Then, like the sun breaking through a cloud,
it was pronounced clear and loud.
All my men turn to see,
if the letter was actually for me.

Each one took his turn handing the mail sack,
all were smiling and patting each other on the back.
The slight rain had smudged the ink,
I held it in my hand not knowing what to think.

It had been months, maybe a year,
the frazzled end of the envelope I begin to tear.
A single red ribbon fell from the inside,
it was kinked and twisted from being untied.

It drifted forever to the ground,
the air around me vanished, there was not a sound.
It had held her hair,
I remember because I tied it there.

I said, "this is what ties you to me,
as long as you wear it, we will always be."
I am not sure if it was the rain or a tear,
that made me realize my deepest fear.

I thought not knowing was a cruelty unmatched,
but little did I realize how much pain can be dispatched.
There were no words needed,
the garden of betrayal had been seeded.

I blamed her then I blamed me,
for the things I didn't see,
her loneliness, the countless nights wondering,
the fear of having to hear the bugles thundering.

The ribbon began to sink into the mud in which it had landed,
being readily accepted by it, just like, when it was first handed.
The heel of my boot finished the submersion as I walked by,
another day in the quagmire, another day living with a lie.

A Sergeant's Cry

In the early morning light,
a sergeant views the grueling sight,
street rubble piled high,
gases escaping the cooling bodies with a sigh!

He checks left and right,
to see the survivors of the night,
all good warriors, all good men,
tears in his heart, and tears for his friend.

In the darkness of night; stealth their friend,
they came!
Sharpness has no sound; death by bayonets is grim,
He hangs his head as he writes another name.

Morning light shows where men fell and died
loss soul's drift into the sky.
He hates death, and war with its endless supply.
His heart breaks, he kneels and cries.

Why have you forsaken him,
in this land of rain,
a river in which he can't swim,
dragged under by the pain?

O' spirit of light, he has escaped death's grasp.
Deliver him from death's eerie song.
He has made no dealings; his time has not elapsed.
He has done no wrong.

Let him go home.

Thousand Mile Eyes

Drifting mist like the soul that prowls,
eyes that portray a thousand miles.
The look of loneliness is what you see,
a heartless person trying not to be.

A long sad journey awaits those who,
consider being with you.
A being of no feeling they do not choose,
A path of no love they do not lose.

For those eyes which tell it all,
deadness in the souls,
like leaves dying in the fall,
thousand mile eyes, are blackened holes.

Their peer is deep and dark,
lost hope, no help, no ark.
The face showing an empty glare,
a hollow stare like mist in the air.

The Same Sound

Like dirty old clothes discarded,
I lay on the floor as we are bombarded,
each explosion shakes the ground,
agonizing seconds before the next round.

The air is filled with bunker dust,
sweat from your fatigues forms a crust,
a piercing sound fills the night,
echoing someone's awful plight.

Pulling myself to the gun port,
making an example of some sort,
seeing nothing but the stars gleaming,
I realize it's me that's screaming.

Why am I hollering,
better yet why am I bothering,
no one can hear,
their ears are closed by fear.

In a moment the shelling ceases,
quietness seeps through the creases,
I don't know when I stopped yelling,
was I the only one, there is no telling.

Looking around at dust covered faces,
standing in boots with untied laces,
you immediately understand,
that sound was coming from every man.

The Drenching of the Soul

The decay of the jungle laces the air,
its pungent odors add to the choking despair.
The pounding rain is relentless like the enemy you chase,
always there but never face to face.

Its wetness is unforgiving and slowly dissolves your hope
it covers you with the mud, it washes down from the slope.
Making each trail impassable, it having been destroyed by
the rain,
it is somewhat ironic because they were just paths to pain.

As it soaks the clothing and envelops the very being
small streaks of it run down the body like your soul fleeing.
It is a form of baptism, a chance to redeem
a spiritual bath with everything wiped clean.

It doesn't last long for there is still a war
and each human evil involved still wants more.
So more bodies are returned to the dust
and it 's the demon, not the rain, that sweeps then away
with a lust.

Concertina Stars

Peering into the night,
concertina wire shining bright,
the gun port framing,
where I was aiming.

The truthful moon,
would show it soon.
No darkness in the field,
exposure means killed.

The jungle immense and thickly,
they emerged from it quickly.
Silhouettes of life,
forcing the strife.

Wait!
See the eyes that hate,
closer even still,
their blood you spill.

Unleashing chaos and grief,
answering death's bequeath.
Darkness beckons them,
in it their souls swim.

Again I am peering,
quietness in the clearing,
points of Concertina Wires,
shining like stars.

Thoughts on Patrol

Alkaline taste from a canteen,
an enemy that goes unseen,
breath sucking heat,
blisters on my feet.

Villages of hollow stares,
living in daily nightmares,
knowing you are hated,
worried about being crated.

Bone drenching rain,
mosquitoes until insane,
nights of quietness,
explosions of brightness.

Never found lost friends,
new faces innocent grins,
another day on the trail,
one step from gates of hell.

Old photos held tight,
peering into a jungle night,
talking to the supreme being,
questioning and disbelieving.

Letters from home,
loved one left alone,
an infant never seen,
must keep weapon clean.

Being lifted by the bird,
remembering her last word,
hoping that it will end,
going out doing it again.

When We Were Thirty

A room we would fill,
full of laughter and bravery,
not worried how war would kill.
We drank to sunlight,
later cried all night,
in the darkness of a bunker.
From boys to men,
with eyes sunken in,
in the middle of a war,
we couldn't win.
When the moment,
came for some,
their mothers were the one,
for which they yelled,
others just laid silent,
as life seeped from them,
what was left, huddled,
in fear for they might be next,
still yet when the challenge came,
they rose up and,
drudged forward never wavering,
in what they had to do,
each one depending on the other,
a brotherhood forged of the past,
so he would survive, he would last.
Yes, when there were thirty of us,
we would fill a room,
we still do,
there's just a little more room,
because a memory only takes
up space in the mind,
I see them now,
laughing, it makes me smile.
I can't wait to be with them again,
I don't know how.
I survived it somehow,
when we were thirty,
now we are three,
please don't let me be the one
to leave the key
to an empty room.

The Burden of When

The bamboo is overpowering,
each stem ominous and towering,
hiding within it, what lies,
an enemy with piercing eyes.

You must not lay still,
become the jungle you will,
pulled down by the vines,
and held captive by twisting tines.

It drips darkness and slime.
You feel its weight,
the burden of fate.
When is my time?

The foliage presses against you,
unwilling to let you through,
resisting what is foreign and strange,
its fights change.

To escape it you must find light,
a clearing not blocking sight,
small wind blowing on the face,
air fresh and without taste.

It is then when you realize,
that no one heard your cries,
except for the enemy, who lies,
in the jungle, with laughing eyes.

Rain of Guilt

A lightning flash exposes a face,
hidden under a dripping brim,
lifeless eyes gives no trace,
of the memories he has within.

A thousand daggers with stinging pain,
is the sensation of the bone chilling rain,
small in comparison to what he feels,
that emptiness in his soul when he kills.

It is a destiny not of his choice,
a future with a contesting voice,
conscious of being misled,
his body stays, the mind long fled.

Another lightning bolt in the night air,
exposing a man very much in despair,
soaked with the rain of guilt,
in the fetal position wrapped in a quilt.

Adapted

Not so tenacious now, are you,
laying there,
dragged out from your tunnel,
a demon's throat filled with putrid air,
in which you lived.
Extracted by one who has adapted,
who will lay in the dark for days if need.
I smelled you, your perspiration,
soaked into the ground in which I laid,
retribution was my deception,
you could not resist it.
I baited you and you came,
like the fly to the web.
I left him there plain for you to see,
just like the ones you left for me.
You were vain and it cost you.
When did you realize it, that exact moment?
That you were mine.
Was it a burning flash in your mind,
or a cold fear running down your spine?
You were good I was better,
I emerge into the sunlight,
from five days of continuous night.
I leave a bicycle card as my mark,
you will take no more of mine,
let the others see,
that there's a hunter,
in the jungle,
who will follow into your lair,
and is at home there,
breathing your putrid air.

Black Angel

The steady drone, the blades continuous whirl,
it all seeps into your mind, making the stomach curl.
The chopper slides through the darkness silently,
in moments it will deliver its message violently.

It delivers death, but not in its true form,
much like lightning is carried by a storm.
Its strike is random; it hunts no particular face,
those in its path will need God's good grace.

The runners strike the ground, and hell opens up,
belching out its rejects to do its bidding.
For the enemy to expect any mercy, themselves they would be
kidding.
They had unknowingly gathered for their last sup.

In just a few black moments, the devastation was done.
The only ones living had chosen to run.
This wasn't for glory, not even a flag to unfurl.
Just like their lives, the dust scattered as the blades begin to whirl.

Lifted into darkness like the angels of death we were,
those short few moments now a blur.
The orange from the fires were glistening very bright,
lighting the way for the lost souls who just took flight.

Tears

Why are we here?
Causing terror and fear,
no business in this place,
that 's not smiles on their face.

We bring more pain,
just like the sickening rain.
You can't trust or believe,
because they will deceive.

They live two lives,
those who survives,
but you can't blame.
You would do the same.

They watch as we walk by,
they have the same question. Why?
I'm a Marine I want to say,
this is where I am told to stay.

At night you dig in,
more and likely it will begin,
those who were peeking.
now come seeking.

As the first flare illuminates the sky,
you realize somewhere a family will cry.
The tears don't pick a side,
they flow for all who have died.

LOST LOVE

Loneliness creeps across my soul

Lost Love

Loneliness creeps across my soul,
like the wind blows across the meadow.
Missing you has no boundaries,
just like a fence that never ends.

The words we use to speak,
now echo hollow and weak.
I now know how fragile love is,
once shattered, you truly miss.

I call out your name to silence.
I never expect a reply.
Any answer I suspect, a lie,
a subconscious thought with malice.

So leave me no hope, I ask in vain,
relieve my heart of its pain.
Do not leave a thread of desire.
Just leave the ashes caused by the fire!

What is Lonely

It is hollowness, with all feelings void,
a loved one lost, a lifetime destroyed.
It may be a decision, to most not a choice,
to come home to a dark house without a voice.

The coldness of a never ending embrace,
but never actually being face to face.
It shields against a touch that ignites flames,
and casts despair on countless faces and names.

It masquerades as being the other side,
alone not lonely, all the while your soul has died.
A thoughtless realm of drifting without hope or meaning,
your mouth is closed but your mind is screaming.

It is a search that never ends for some,
because what they found turns out to be no one.
A faction of life others have adapted to,
being happy, only a seldom few.

It truly is a quest of fortitude and survival,
and is not welcomed upon its arrival.
A transparency of the mirrors reflection,
a ghost of a person trying to make a connection.

Storm of Emotions

The cumulus hordes the sky with it overpowering dominance,
blending the wind, light, and rain to create its earthly ambiance.
The darkness reflecting the spirit of my mood,
a lighting flash exposing a soul that needs soothed.

Within its cavernous body, eruptions of sound echo loudly,
mimicking a newborn announcing itself to the world proudly.
A crescendo that builds to the intensity of a freight train,
and then it is quieted by the wind blowing sheets of rain.

The next chorus starts where the last one ended,
creating the desired affect the first had intended.
Lighting lashes out with no particular direction,
wherever it strikes has very little protection.

In a unique chaotic way it simulates love in every way,
creating attention to itself like a strutting peacock on display.
A bolt to the heart leaving one's emotions shocked and suspended,
and just as fast as it started, another flash and it has ended.

The quiet after the storm is a lonely period of seeking,
that leaves one searching for answers and self critiquing.
As children we hurried into the rain to play,
as adults confronting love, we seem to run the other way.

Recovering

You say I never loved you,
that I broke your heart in two.
Good! It needed to bleed,
it was full of impurities and greed.

Like the flood being held by the wall,
hardly no emotion seeped from you at all.
So let your heart drip its coldness,
it pleasures me in my newfound boldness.

Seeing you languish in sorrow,
no friends with sympathy to borrow.
That black heart dying,
from all the poison and lying.

I am removed from you now,
and in time, again I will smile.
For my heart was broken too,
but unlike yours, it was love that spew.

DEATH

What we seek from birth

Remembering

Our greatest test and pleasure is life,
it being divided between love and strife.
To lose love so abruptly and cruel,
should never be considered a rule.

In their memories is where you must find strength,
doing whatever to find comfort at any length.
Remember their love for you,
for it is what will carry you through.

In the long days and nights that follow,
your emotions will list and be hollow,
remember them and they will be there,
helping you with your despair.

Your feelings for them will always be the bond,
that you call upon when all other is gone.
You have not lost them, they are with you,
their love for you is ageless, as is yours too!

It is that time in your life,
where you are tested by strife,
and as it is said on the lines above,
you will survive because you have their love.

The Devil's Dove

For days now you have sat and peered,
not leaving once, keeping up your continuous jeer.
Is your heart as black as your plumage,
a vestment of death looking for a soul to rummage.

Is it I you have chosen, you fiend,
perched out there like you're unseen.
Are you the same who haunted Poe,
driving him crazy ever so slow.

You are not wanted here, that I am aware,
no invitation to you and your deadly stare.
If it is a soul you want, find another,
This house has surrendered a father and brother.

If that is truly what you are,
an instrument of the relentless reaper.
Your menacing presence looking from afar,
causing the fear in my heart to go even deeper.

And if you are not what you seem,
a messenger who has come to do a deed.
My warning you should greatly heed,
fly from me now, you evil thing with a gleam.

I will strike at you with all my might,
putting an end to that hollow sight.
So now I have made the game a new.
Maybe it is I who has came for you!

Coldness of Death

Standing beside the frozen eternal resting place,
listening to the pastor expound on God's grace.
The coldness of the wind penetrating deep,
not as shivering as hearing the mother weep.

Before me lie memories, now neatly contained,
beside me my friend, battling to stay sane.
The things in life that matter, really don't,
never forgetting my friend's suffering, I won't.

His words were brave, and strongly said,
"Its a miserable day to bury our dead."
As an answer to give, I only had one,
"Any day is miserable, you bury a son."

As the casket was lowered into the ground,
sadness and sorrow was the only sound.
Two lives were lost this day of grim,
sadden, knowing that my friend's life just dimmed.

I hope that I never experience this,
I want to be first.
A parent shouldn't be the last to exist,
dying couldn't be as worse.

Dead Man's Shirt

The shirts were freshly starched,
wrapped in cellophane,
the shoes polished, straight in line and plain,
each one blocked protecting the arch.

The trouser legs all folded to the left side,
and pulled down halfway, and squared with pride.
The suit jackets were buttoned and pressed,
ready to be worn when he was to be put to rest.

The belts were all curled and laying on the shelf,
the socks were folded and placed as if they had wealth.
Every tie was hung on the rack,
all the sweaters piled high in a colorful stack.

I slipped a shirt from its hangar using great care,
pulling it on, something normally I wouldn't dare.
No need to worry now, he is not here.
Standing in front of the mirror my eyes begin to tear.

I now understand why things had to be his way,
everything in order and him having the last say.
I deliberately caused him humility, pain and hurt,
recognizing it now, wearing this dead man's shirt.

Pondering's of an Old Man

His face is quite wrinkled now and he stares with a squint.
He has a slow canter, brought about, because his back is so bent.
The fingers of his hands are gnarled, like driftwood roots laying on
the shore,
the numbing pain in them he has learned to ignore.

These last years have not been kind to him.
It was a picture all too clear, his life was starting to dim,
first taking his wife and leaving him alone.
It was a life in which he no longer wanted to belong.

His thoughts were about the sunrises,
his memories were about her,
she always was laughing and full of surprises,
as he laid his head down they become a blur.

Awaking to another day, he is saddened and grieved,
if he did not awake he would have been relieved.
His eyes would not have to see the pain of another day,
he could just lay there and watch his soul be carried away.

Growing Old

The dead tree bends to the wind,
it is a bow of dignity.
A gesture of humbleness,
an acknowledgment, not a sin.

Its life, now extinguished.
Its seed no longer spread,
its sap long been bled.
An unworthy sad finish!

Much like this pine,
I am one of its kind.
Life's creeping slow pace,
the wind caressing my face.

The sun brings more decay,
just like dying has its agonizing way.
Ending as the same,
from whence we came.

Born from birth,
roots to earth.
It cries no sound,
the body let down.

Routine

The kitchen clock chimes that it is five,
she sets two cups of coffee at the table,
like she always has as if he still was alive.
Any moment now she will hear him out in the stable.

She patiently waits for the turn of the handle,
and him to enter, placing his hat above the mantle.
On the stove the evening meal is prepared,
her preparations are perfect nothing is spared.

For thirty years she has loved this man,
why he hasn't come in, she doesn't understand.
She walks to the window and pulls back the shade.
All she can see is where he has been laid.

LIFE

Just a brief moment in this world

Winter of Life

Winter extends its hands asking,
the trees resist but give,
leaves laying in the sun basking.
One whole summer they have lived.

Joined by the wind with its wisps,
they move about in disarray.
Morning air, crystal and crisp,
has taken them this winter day.

This parity I see in life,
the cycle, as I complete my path,
brings me before him to face his wrath,
a final ending of my strife.

Warmth has given way to cold.
Living to dying,
youth to old.
Like the leaves, I wait for it, lying.

Winter extends its hand asking,
I resist!
There is more than everlasting.
The coming of spring, reasons to exist.

Dark Mountains

Weathered shack on the side of the hill,
inside people, who have lost their will.
Government commodities on their plate,
a life of poverty is their fate.

Hid away at the end of a hollow,
the children have no one to follow,
so it repeats itself once more,
another generation learning to be poor.

No shoes on dirty little feet,
hunger of the mind being beat,
a look of lost in their eyes,
no one notices when the spark dies.

These mountains so beautiful, hides a lot,
with people living there, sharing not,
as they stand the test of time,
what goes unnoticed is a devastating crime.

To escape the trend of giving in,
requires a spirit not willing to bend.
From the mountains it must flee,
shedding the darkness of ignorance to be free.

The Fight From Within

Agonizing, terrible lonely pain,
it plagues me with no rest.
Like shivers from a winter rain,
it is my body, it has chosen to infest.

My cries are silent, lost on the wind.
The heart pulsing out of control,
from the sickness that is within,
nothing is spared not even my soul.

Fighting the urge to stand and to shout,
I must find the serenity of peace,
and do away with self doubt.
My will to live I will increase.

I pry life from darkness,
a grasp which holds death.
I am alive not extinguished.
I go forward, each step a new breath.

I am victorious, a warrior of the soul.
My body my castle, even if it is old.
I will not surrender or waver, it is my quest.
If I would happen to fail, you will have had my best.

Change

I saw you today for the first time,
not as that giggling, smiling, happy little boy,
but as a young man, in his prime,
fully aware, it 's time to lay down his toy.

As you stood before me, with her holding your hand,
I recognized your gentleness and smile.
It was obvious; you had confidence and style,
her love for you I understand.

When did it start this transition?
Was youth wisp away by the wind,
or like snow melting, a slow attrition?
Where was I when it began?

Was I a proper guiding light?
Giving you direction and insight,
I'm not sure about the things I've done.
Was I there when you needed me son?

The man I see before me I like,
I acknowledge his passage to manhood,
he no longer needs my might.
He speaks for himself now as he should.

For the Innocent Children

It was a demon that ravished her mind,
put there by a man being "kind."
There would never be a man she could trust,
having suffered the indignities of a predator's lust.

He would visit her in the darkness of night,
when all things where silent and quiet.
The horrors of what he done,
shouldn't be suffered by anyone.

Innocence stolen, nightmares embedded,
all hope of normalcy has been shredded.
Behind her eyes is hollowness and despair,
in her heart, solidity, harden without a care.

With any luck there still might be a glimmer,
one thing that wouldn't make her chances slimmer.
A small particle of desire and resolute,
the willingness to stop him from finding another recruit.

In this passion for her vengeance of restitution,
she found life and meaningfulness, a solution.
She had become an avenging angel, wiping out sin.
feeling whole again, her soul not scattered to the wind.

They visited him in the darkness, instead of the day,
because it was what she wanted, it was his way.
All things were silent and quiet,
except for the horrors that took place that night.

The demon he had spawned was of his kind,
it knew what to do to destroy his mind.
It left him babbling and crying out in the wild,
no longer will he be a hunter of the child.

The Old Swimming Hole

Having raced and getting there first,
winning nothing but what it was worth.
The one to wet my soul before another could,
since I won, it would be only proper that I should.

Pulling down the straps of my Blue Jack Denims,
over my shoulder I see the rushing Billy Cremins.
I drop to the ground and pull off my brogans,
the dust from them causes a cloud that covers my hands.

I tossed them to the side and the knickers came next,
one more look I saw Billy throwing his belted school text.
I jumped to my feet and pulled my wool over my head,
Billy ran by, I never heard what he said.

The only thing left was my cotton white shorts,
flying through the air, like a great surrendering flag, if we'd been
playing forts.
Another quick step and I had the rope in my grip,
pulling it back, then I ran forward, holding tight as not to slip.

The old tree limb bent with my weight,
causing that feeling in my stomach that I hate.
It lifted me up toward the sun and for a moment we were one.
Letting go and flying through the air, my body goes numb.

As I submerge into the water, blackness surrounded me,
the coolness cascades over my body and in that moment, I am free.
Bursting through the surface, gasping for air,
all I can hear is Billy Cremins hollering, "Not fair."

Fire

It is a mindless, engulfing wall of flame.
First this house then the next,
destroying all; just the same,
aligning with the wind to be complex.

It 's the devil 's lapping tongue,
his breathe creates a crust.
It burns everything with a lust.
Its crackling a song being sung.

The blackened ground its trail.
Charred remains its mark,
pungent air its smell,
destroyed dreams from a spark.

A cleansing of the earth,
something we don't understand.
Even the things we give worth,
can't get a helping hand.

We are at its mercy, when it 's our turn.
An enemy without a heart,
a soul of vengeance that needs to burn.
An evil we can't depart.

From the heavens from which it came,
a streaking mystical deadly pain.
From the heavens we need the same,
mystical droplets of falling rain.

Questionable Believer

It seems humans need something on a larger scope.
Is it a weakness of mankind to need hope?
Is it necessary to have a common bond,
something giving guidance from out there and beyond?

If my very being exists on the fact that I must
succumb to the ways of others, surrendering my trust,
then I have lost more than my soul before I even start.
I would be nothing if I didn't believe in the purity of my
heart.

If I am to be controlled and expected to refrain,
then there should be no discomfort, sickness, or pain.
These things have not yet happened, and neither have I.
Wars are still happening and children still die.

If it is I who you want to cross over and be on bended knee,
then stop all of this devastation that I see.
Maybe for an almighty power it is an impossible feat,
but until then I will continue to stand on my own two feet.

ROMANCE

If romance is a road to be traveled,
Then I have traveled very far,
for I have known love

Light into the Night

Like a stone cast upon the water,
my heart skips when you are near,
Your essence captivates my senses,
making each one a slave to you.

The smoothness of your skin,
like shifting silky desert sand,
eased along by the wind,
arousing sensations deep from within.

Your kindness is my sun,
your beauty my stars,
I will never know loneliness,
while they shine from afar.

It is you that makes my day,
in every way,
that makes sense and what 's right,
you are my light into the night.

Morning Quietness

Through the window comes the morning ray,
highlighting your beauty as you lay.
I count each breath as you sleep.
So happy you're beside me, it makes me weep.

This love I want, no reason to resist,
I have found my answer to exist.
How I feel, I have nothing to compare,
It 's voluminous, void of air.

I stroke your hand, I caress the face.
The outline of your lips my fingers trace.
The softness allows my heart pleasure,
and are emotions greater than any treasure.

These feelings I only knew,
as the mornings shine from above.
These moments are my time with you,
and are the moments when I fall in love.

Surrender

The limbs of the tree are barren now,
like a face that does not smile,
picked clean by the wind with each blow,
like a heart that has lost its soul.

Removing love from your life,
is like losing the leaves.
All is left is a naked strife,
which brings you to your knees.

To find that one light,
that makes you glow,
that feels so right,
a true love to know.

You must search, but not in vain,
cheating loneliness, to ease the pain.
You must be smart,
in saving your heart.

The feelings of the heart, so thin,
to offer it once again,
exposing it to the wind.
If its love, you must give in!

Loves Gleam

It is the beacon of desire,
for the lonely caught in a quagmire.
Its rays of light are arms of salvation,
reaching to those dying of love starvation.

If I should be so lucky that it would shine on me,
my spirit would truly be set free.
Should it cast over me,
leaving my soul in the dark, so shall it be.

HOLIDAYS

Of all the inventions of man,
Holidays was the best,
because they arouse emotions of all kinds

Veteran

The significant of that first shot,
was more than a loud sound.
It was defiance, surrender not,
America's first veterans standing ground.

Since that time, no matter the strife,
providing freedom their concern.
Gladly surrendering their life,
expecting nothing in return.

They come when asked.
Standing the line,
ready for the task,
leaving family behind.

For reasons so clear,
and not hard to understand.
Not to live in fear,
and protecting the land.

So the next time you impose your right.
Be it speak out, vote, or protest.
Recognize the guy who allowed you to gripe.
My guess; he has ribbons on his chest.

It does not need to be said,
but I am willing to bet.
At night; when you're safely in bed.
You can thank a Vet!

Semper Fi!
Veteran

July 4th, 1776

Richard Lee's resolution to declare,
a challenge to others who may dare.
Jefferson to task with pen in hand,
Dunlap's broadsides spread through the land.

The Boston massacre was a fact,
then came the Sugar and Quartering Act.
The crown of tyranny set ships a sail,
in Charleston they waited to repel.

Thirteen colonies against an empire,
they have might, we had desire.
So on a cool day in a Philadelphia hall,
fifty six men signed their names standing tall.

Declaring their unalienable right,
and willing to die in the fight,
being sequestered an unwillingness,
all for life, liberty, and pursuit of happiness.

Two hundred thirty two years a free land,
all because brave men took a stand.
Now in these days of discontent,
how many know what it really meant.

In Honor of Pearl

In they flew wave after wave,
each sailor trying, his ship to save.
Just like their flag they came at sunrise,
catching our boys totally by surprise.

In they flew wave after wave,
Zeke's, Val's and Cates, all carrying deadly fate,
by the time we knew, it was too late,
mighty ships sinking to their grave.

In they flew wave after wave,
bombs finding targets, something they crave.
The devastation was starting to amass,
how much longer could this last.

In they flew wave after wave,
this Sunday no souls will be saved.
Our men resisting wherever they could.
Why the attack, no one understood.

In they flew wave after wave,
with the smoke clogging the air,
and the bodies filling the water,
trying to finish an all out slaughter.

In they flew wave after wave,
many injured, thousands lay dead.
It was explained by the man who led,
"A date which will live in Infamy"

In Honor of those brave military people,
who endured while being in harm's way.

Mother's Voice

As an infant my memories were few,
the sensations I felt were vibrant and new.
My life existed around very little choice,
but I would lay silent just to hear her voice.

The wind would snap the freshly hung laundry,
to a young boy in the yard this always caused a quandary,
how could she work so hard and still hum that chorus,
but I would always stop playing just to hear her voice.

It is of her character that I am a blend,
she was not only my mother, she was my friend,
when I left home I still remember her lips so moist,
and how it felt just to hear her voice.

It has been years now since she went away,
I think of her often, not a moment passes in the day.
From the moment I first remember to the casket I had to hoist,
What I wouldn't give for one more time just to hear her voice.

Coming Home

Little faces a glow,
Angels made in the snow.
Smells of home from the stove,
well worth the miles you drove.

The tree decorated in its splendor,
the pictures mounted on the hearth.
The memories they bring so tender,
not remembering wearing that scarf!

The hunt where you don't shoot,
this might be his last time,
to the kids it the loot,
he is well past his prime.

The meal to her was no bother,
just an offering from our father.
This might be her last time,
she is well past her prime.

Songs sang with spirit,
tears and heart tugs.
So happy to hear it,
the laughter and hugs.

Yes it is the season,
that message like a drone,
letting me know the reason,
for why I'm coming home.

My Christmas Poem

My soul is shining like the stars at night,
just like long ago, a guiding light.
It is not a gift from three wise men,
but love coming, deep from within.

It is happiness, no jewelry could adorn,
just like nothing could match him being born.
A heart beating, love cannot be denied,
staying in a manger, not below their pride.

It was a silent night, the sheep covered with dew,
the world's hope was coming, the beginning of new.
His arrival such a welcomed thing,
the gates of heaven opened and the angels began to sing.

The golden trumpets bellowed a blare,
the shepherds stood with an astonished stare.
This night of birth,
when the Savior came to earth.

This time we honor, by acknowledging him,
with deeds like peace on earth,
good will to men.
These are the gifts you need to send.

Christmas Feelings

All the children in their seat, anxiously moving their feet,
they know it 's Christmas time here on earth.
A time of snow, wind, and sleet,
It 's a celebration, it 's joy, it 's all about the birth.

From the heavens the angels sing,
little children hang their stockings with a gleam.
A warmth from the fireplace, good for the soul,
melting sadness from the heart, like frost on the window.

A metal train with whistles and lanterns that really glows,
Red-haired rag dolls made out of socks with a button nose.
Secret wishes only the children and Santa knows,
just like who sneaked and kissed who under the mistletoe.

In the darkness the church bell rings,
aided by the wind the holy sound it brings.
The trees and holly bushes, covered in star light, all a glisten,
add to the beauty as I stand and listen.

In the distance I see the village lanterns all in line,
just like for Jesus, the stars above brightly shine.
It is the Holy Spirit riding on the moonlight,
there is no fear, only joy on this night.

For this night I wish happiness forever,
good will to all men,
may they find peace from within,
and the love they seek, a rewarding endeavor.

Christmas Lemon Tree

In a milk carton at the age of three,
he told me he was planting his Christmas tree.
For years I watched it grow,
he ensured me growing Christmas was slow.

When he decided that it was ready,
he tied it to a stick to make it steady.
He drug out a box and started to adorn,
all the while humming about Jesus being born.

All these things I am happy to see,
hanging from my lemon Christmas tree.
There are the ice sickles from aluminum foil.
The eight-sided star, the labors of his toil.

The clay thing he dried in the sun,
no matter the paint had melted and run.
The stick men, from straws he had twisted,
they were elves, I remember he had insisted.

The snowman from the number eight,
melting would have been a kinder fate.
And the best, for last, so all could see.
His cut out angel at the top of the
lemon Christmas tree.

NATURE

*A person only needs to look to
find ones being*

The Pond

As a child I had a place of which I was very fond.
It wasn't much, just an old farm pond.
One evening I decided to visit it and found it grown over and
dense.
My eyes strained to see as I slipped through the barbed wire fence.

I first noticed the saw grass stems that rocketed toward the sky.
Each one a streamer bringing remembrance of the Fourth of July.
The Magpies zipped in and out as they flew by.
In the background you can hear the Katydids cry.

The lily pads floated together, each one an island of solitude.
From them come the songs of the frogs, boisterous and crude.
The sound drifts across the water mixed with the evening fog.
A startled water turtle slips off his sunning log.

The water mosquitoes dance their crazy dance.
Below the surface, patient, shell crackers waiting their chance.
The muskrat has disappeared; the remaining tracks its only trace.
The wind ripples the water creating wrinkles like on an old
person's face.

The moon hiding in one corner has chosen to be shy.
Covering only the small end of the pond where the cattails lie.
Two mallards swoop low giving the pond a final test.
Making sure that this haven will offer a good night 's rest.

Their landing disrupts the fishing of a Sandhill Crane.
His departure was noisy and his squawking profane.
As he circled to gain a comfortable flying height,
the darkness closed in, bringing the pond into the night.

Even though I had grown old and have poor sight,
I could still see it all.
For it has been in my mind every night,
since I was very small.

The Vigil

A light drizzle settles the dust.
A Whippoorwill whoops for lust.
The rain puddles among the rows.
It 's a good day the farmer knows.

Deers peek from the woods,
being cautious as they should.
Before them lies the evening meal,
mist from the rain causing an eerie still.

A lone crow crosses in the wind.
His lonely caw inquiring for a friend.
His black feathers slick from the rain,
in the distance another echoes his pain.

A lightning flash highlights the corn,
it 's a signal for all to be forewarned.
In the field is not a place to be,
the farmer hides and waits to see.

He knows that his crop is the treasure.
His hard work won't be another's pleasure.
On his hat the rain beats the brim,
causing a chill that covers him.

The day gives way to dark.
The Whippoorwill is replaced by a lark.
The crow has long gone.
The deer and the farmer wait for dawn.

Tempting Meadow

Standing above the meadow all covered with life,
I found a small path cutting through the middle like a knife.
It was lined with the Crested Dog Tail plant,
and crisscrossed with the many trails of the meadow ant.

Fluttering from Butter Cups, Cocks Foot, and Nest Nettles,
an undecided Marble White tries to settle.
The Bush Crickets keep up their rhythmic sing,
all the while laying harbored by the Orchid Green Wing.

As I meander down this maze of thistle and foliage,
I try to be careful as not to add man's touch or spoilage.
Reaching the end, I am greeted with a gallery of Ragged Robbins,
all gathered at the waters edge with beautiful Demoiselles bobbin.

I could not resist the temptation of kicking off my shoes,
walking in the water and watching the sand between my toes ooze.
I sat down making a bed of the Yellow Rattle that is guarded by
the Peacock butterflies.
I fell asleep watching Golden-Ringed Dragons, etch their signature
flights in the blue skies.

The Lion's Tooth

Like the Knight on his steed ready to charge into battle,
I have picked my park bench and sit astraddle.
Before me lies the land of the lions tooth,
I hunt it to make a simple elixir not a Chateauneuf.

The evening dew sparkling on the rayed yellow head,
with its notched basal leave, will let you be mislead.
For you think your fingers it will prick,
another one of nature's way, the predator to trick.

The sun highlights the brilliant and vivid yellow,
falsely pulling you toward Elysian fields of mellow,
creating inner cravings to lay amongst them and bask,
all the while forgetting about your harvesting task.

But I set staunch on my noble steed,
for my appetite is whetted and I am determined to feed,
this night on fresh salads made from the Dandelion,
while waiting a fortnight to taste the lions tooth, made into
wine.

Dancing with Mother Nature

The wheat in the meadows sways with the wind,
a majestic dance with the sun joining in.
The birds add to the ramble with their darting in and out,
the trees at the end of the field with limbs whipping about.

The clouds in the sky slowly waltz their way by.
It is a mixture of movement you can not deny.
You feel your feet slowly begin to move,
your body moving, getting in a groove.

That last gust of wind does the trick.
You take that first step and hear your heels click.
You swirl and tilt your head toward the sky,
dancing with Mother Nature allows you to fly.

When the dance ends and you float gently down,
with your feet still swirling around.
What a feeling to have on such a windy day,
being invited by nature to dance and play.

Full Moon

The orb, mystical and unique,
it commands the wolf and demands he speak.
A crescent smile with a changing face,
all the while holding the shadow in its place.

Its silver light cascading down to earth,
creating a connection to a few,
who where blessed by birth,
while it was in full view.

Like the tides of the ocean,
their souls are pulled back and forth.
A constant wave of emotion,
like the unrelenting beckoning to fly from the north.

Visiting the celestial waters of blue,
to celebrate its coming, its wholesome anew.
Its greatness, they exude,
by submersing themselves totally nude.

It has caused man to reach and try,
and when blue, bring tears to the eye.
A word written in so many tunes,
no wonder we like Full Moons.

Bio

Having been born in West Virginia and growing up in the Appalachian Mountains during impoverished times, it gave me a different look at life than most young people will ever grasp. The reality of being separated from family and raised by others and never ever knowing who your father was had a long and devastating effect on me until I was able to deal with it. The Marines did what they do best and they set me on a straight and narrow course. Having survived and once again on my own, I attended college and worked. The seed of discontent and unsettlement had been sewn and I jumped around from job to job and state to state and finally ended up in North Carolina. An attempt at marriage failed but left the one thing most precious to me in the world … my son. If not having been for him, it is unimaginable as to where I would have ended up and what kind of condition I would be in. I have always wanted to write and made several attempts. The world is an interesting place and all you have to do is observe.